Life Worth Living

A DAILY GROWTH JOURNAL

KRISTIN VANDERLIP

Life Worth Living: A Daily Growth Journal
Copyright © 2019 by Kristin Vanderlip
Cover Design by Kristin Vanderlip
All rights reserved.

Find Kristin Vanderlip on the web here:
Website: KristinVanderlip.com
Instagram: KristinVanderlip
Facebook: kristinvanderlipwriter

Published in the USA
ISBN: 9781092975605

This journal belongs to:

_____

Date:

_02/11/20_____

A note for you

While I might not know you personally, I do know that you and your life have significant worth. You are more than your highs and more than your lows. You have been wonderfully and uniquely created,[1] you are perfectly loved,[2] and there is an abundant life worth living for you.[3]

Do you know that? My guess is that you're struggling to believe that. Maybe you think there are too many obstacles or there is too much pain or there is too much wrong with you or your life. Maybe you feel like you're constantly struggling and desperately feel weary from the struggle. Maybe you feel stuck. Maybe your world isn't how you wanted it to be or thought it would be. Maybe you feel like the color is draining right out of your life.

Perhaps you're here and you're grieving the death of someone close to you. Maybe you're walking through the loss of a relationship or trying to work through a difficult one. Maybe you're wrestling with overwhelming feelings of sorrow, abandonment, resentment, discontentment, or something else. Maybe you've experienced a form of trauma. Maybe old patterns of behaviors and thoughts are no longer serving you and you're ready to see them transformed.

I don't know the details of your struggle, but I do know that we all struggle. Sometimes life is hard. Sometimes life hurts. Sometimes life seems overwhelming. And sometimes we feel like a bystander as we watch our life fade away into a bleak, gray landscape. But, we long for the return of a vibrant and flourishing life. We long for a renewed spirit and the return of hope.

The beautiful thing is that abundant living is ours for the taking, but it won't come without winning some battles first. You're here because deep down you know this. You're ready for transformation and growth. You're ready to overcome your struggles and break unhealthy cycles. You're in need of a practical boost to propel you forward. I hope this journal will be a tangible tool that will help you win your battles, live as the conqueror you are,[4] and embrace your life that is so worth living.

This journal was birthed out of a personal need in my own life. After spending years in the space of stuck and struggling and longing for growth and overcoming, I wanted a journal to help me with my soul work. The problem was that the type of journal I needed didn't exist. I am not an expert, but I did have a few helpful handouts and resources from licensed therapists and psychologists as well as some wonderful ideas and strategies acquired from various books I'd read over the years. I took all I had learned and what I was looking for and made my own journal. I created and used these journal templates on a daily basis, and this practice became (and still is) essential to my personal growth and well-being.

As you use this journal, I hope that you too will find growth and come alive to your life. So please, come as you are, this space is for you. It's my privilege and honor to be invited on this journey with you as you discover your life worth living.

Blessings,

Kristin

---

[1] See Psalm 139:14
[2] See Psalm 36:7, Jeremiah 31:3, Romans 5:8, Ephesians 2:4-5
[3] See John 10:10, Luke 12:6-7, Ephesians 2:10
[4] See Romans 8:35-37

How to use this journal

Before you get started...

Commit to and set aside time to use this journal *daily*. Growth happens over time and comes with repeated practices that turn into habits.

Read through the Growth Tools sections. Begin by identifying your current struggles and the areas you'd like to see growth in. Discover tools to use in your life. Then go through the Affirmations, Values, Joy in the Small Things, and Awaken My Soul sections to lay some important groundwork for your journey.

Daily journaling...

The first half of your journal contains daily journal pages (you'll find a sample page filled in before your daily pages begin). Each daily journal page includes the following sections:

Daily Check-In—This section offers space for a quick check-in with yourself and functions as an easy reference for reflection. In this space you'll make note of your mood, diet and hydration, energy level, exercise, quiet time (time spent in God's Word and prayer), and a blank space for anything else you want to track. Keeping track of these areas can help you see how they impact your overall wellness.

The Struggles—Use this space to record and describe what you're struggling with that day. It's important to have an awareness and a safe space to get all of the hard "stuff" outside of yourself.

The Growth & Overcoming—What growth or overcoming did you notice in your day? In this space make note of what growth tools you tried and which ones were helpful. Give yourself freedom to try new things and give yourself credit for trying even if the tool didn't seem to help. Tip: Try to match each struggle with at least one growth tool. For more ideas, check out the list of Additional Recommended Resources on the last page of the journal.

The Good List—Here you'll record all of the good in your day. You can think of this as your space to create a gratitude list. The more you practice noticing the good, the more you'll notice your mind rewiring your thought patterns and the color coming back into your life.

Notes—Use this space to make a quick note about anything extra from your day that didn't seem to fit anywhere else. You can record something significant about the day that you want to remember or set an intention for the next day. Use this space however you like.

For growth and going deeper...

Progress Points—These pages appear after every 14 daily journal pages. Progress Points offer you a place to pause your daily journal habit and process your progress. Each page contains a series of questions to help you reflect and move forward. Please don't get bogged down by the word "progress." Sometimes we take 2 steps forward and 1 step back. It's okay! This is not about striving. This is about your life worth living right where you are.

Revelations—The second half of your journal contains a section of blank, bullet-journal style pages. These Revelations pages are designed to offer you free space to record deeper thoughts, prayers, lessons you're learning, goals for yourself, and those "ah ha" revelations that will come. Use these pages to go deeper whenever and however you like.

Daily Journal

S   (M)   T   W   T   F   S

JAN   FEB   MAR   APR   (MAY)   JUNE   JULY   AUG   SEPT   OCT   NOV   DEC

1 2 3 4 5 6 7 8 9 (10) 11 12 13 14 15 16 17 18 19 20 21 22 23 24 25 26 27 28 29 30 31

Daily Check-In

Mood: *anxious*	Exercise: (y) n
Diet / Hydration: *caffeine / 12 oz of water*	Quiet time: y (n)
Energy level: *low------------X------------------high*	_____

The Struggles

- Snapped at the kids before school
- My to-do list is overwhelming me
- I can't seem to shake this sadness lately; I think it has to do with the anniversary of my dad's death approaching

The Growth & Overcoming

- I apologized and practiced radical acceptance with how I treated the kids this morning — focus on moving forward in connection with them.
- I did 5 minutes of breathing exercises while driving in the car to work (this really helped).
- It's possible the caffeine in my coffee and PMS are affecting me today.
- Prioritized the items on my to-do list and asked for help.
- Made some time to do something I enjoyed (reading my new book).

The Good List

- Family hug this afternoon
- Found the book I wanted to read on sale
- Sweet text message from a friend
- Heard my favorite song on the radio
- Watching the sunset on the porch

Notes

Be mindful of my emotions and needs with the grief anniversary approaching. Allow my sorrow space but put a boundary around it. Find a positive way to remember.

S   M   T   W   T   F   S

JAN   FEB   MAR   APR   MAY   JUNE   JULY   AUG   SEPT   OCT   NOV   DEC

1 2 3 4 5 6 7 8 9 10 11 12 13 14 15 16 17 18 19 20 21 22 23 24 25 26 27 28 29 30 31

Daily Check-In

Mood:	Exercise: y n
Diet / Hydration:	Quiet time: y n
Energy level: *low-------------------------------high*	_____

The Struggles

The Growth & Overcoming

The Good List

Notes

S M T W T F S

JAN FEB MAR APR MAY JUNE JULY AUG SEPT OCT NOV DEC
1 2 3 4 5 6 7 8 9 10 11 12 13 14 15 16 17 18 19 20 21 22 23 24 25 26 27 28 29 30 31

Daily Check-In

Mood:	Exercise: y n
Diet / Hydration:	Quiet time: y n
Energy level: *low*----------------------------------*high*	_____

The Struggles

The Growth & Overcoming

The Good List

Notes

S M T W T F S
JAN FEB MAR APR MAY JUNE JULY AUG SEPT OCT NOV DEC
1 2 3 4 5 6 7 8 9 10 11 12 13 14 15 16 17 18 19 20 21 22 23 24 25 26 27 28 29 30 31

Daily Check-In

Mood:	Exercise: y n
Diet / Hydration:	Quiet time: y n
Energy level: *low-------------------------------high*	_____

The Struggles

The Growth & Overcoming

The Good List

Notes

S   M   T   W   T   F   S

JAN FEB MAR APR MAY JUNE JULY AUG SEPT OCT NOV DEC

1 2 3 4 5 6 7 8 9 10 11 12 13 14 15 16 17 18 19 20 21 22 23 24 25 26 27 28 29 30 31

Daily Check-In

Mood:	Exercise: y n
Diet / Hydration:	Quiet time: y n
Energy level: *low------------------------------high*	_____

The Struggles

The Growth & Overcoming

The Good List

Notes

S   M   T   W   T   F   S

JAN   FEB   MAR   APR   MAY   JUNE   JULY   AUG   SEPT   OCT   NOV   DEC

1 2 3 4 5 6 7 8 9 10 11 12 13 14 15 16 17 18 19 20 21 22 23 24 25 26 27 28 29 30 31

Daily Check-In

Mood:	Exercise: y n
Diet / Hydration:	Quiet time: y n
Energy level: *low------------------------------high*	

The Struggles

The Growth & Overcoming

The Good List

Notes

S   M   T   W   T   F   S

JAN   FEB   MAR   APR   MAY   JUNE   JULY   AUG   SEPT   OCT   NOV   DEC

1 2 3 4 5 6 7 8 9 10 11 12 13 14 15 16 17 18 19 20 21 22 23 24 25 26 27 28 29 30 31

Daily Check-In

Mood:	Exercise: y n
Diet / Hydration:	Quiet time: y n
Energy level: *low*-------------------------------*high*	_____

The Struggles

The Growth & Overcoming

The Good List

Notes

S   M   T   W   T   F   S
JAN   FEB   MAR   APR   MAY   JUNE   JULY   AUG   SEPT   OCT   NOV   DEC
1 2 3 4 5 6 7 8 9 10 11 12 13 14 15 16 17 18 19 20 21 22 23 24 25 26 27 28 29 30 31

Daily Check-In

Mood:	Exercise: y n
Diet / Hydration:	Quiet time: y n
Energy level: *low-------------------------------high*	_____

The Struggles

The Growth & Overcoming

The Good List

Notes

S   M   T   W   T   F   S

JAN   FEB   MAR   APR   MAY   JUNE   JULY   AUG   SEPT   OCT   NOV   DEC

1 2 3 4 5 6 7 8 9 10 11 12 13 14 15 16 17 18 19 20 21 22 23 24 25 26 27 28 29 30 31

Daily Check-In

Mood:	Exercise: y n
Diet / Hydration:	Quiet time: y n
Energy level: *low*-------------------------------*high*	_____

The Struggles

The Growth & Overcoming

The Good List

Notes

S M T W T F S

JAN FEB MAR APR MAY JUNE JULY AUG SEPT OCT NOV DEC

1 2 3 4 5 6 7 8 9 10 11 12 13 14 15 16 17 18 19 20 21 22 23 24 25 26 27 28 29 30 31

Daily Check-In

Mood:	Exercise:　　　y　　　n
Diet / Hydration:	Quiet time:　　　y　　　n
Energy level: *low------------------------------high*	_____

The Struggles

The Growth & Overcoming

The Good List

Notes

S   M   T   W   T   F   S
JAN   FEB   MAR   APR   MAY   JUNE   JULY   AUG   SEPT   OCT   NOV   DEC
1 2 3 4 5 6 7 8 9 10 11 12 13 14 15 16 17 18 19 20 21 22 23 24 25 26 27 28 29 30 31

Daily Check-In

Mood:	Exercise: y n
Diet / Hydration:	Quiet time: y n
Energy level: *low*-------------------------------*high*	_____

The Struggles

The Growth & Overcoming

The Good List

Notes

S   M   T   W   T   F   S

JAN FEB MAR APR MAY JUNE JULY AUG SEPT OCT NOV DEC

1 2 3 4 5 6 7 8 9 10 11 12 13 14 15 16 17 18 19 20 21 22 23 24 25 26 27 28 29 30 31

Daily Check-In

Mood:	Exercise: y n
Diet / Hydration:	Quiet time: y n
Energy level: *low------------------------------high*	_____

The Struggles

The Growth & Overcoming

The Good List

Notes

S M T W T F S

JAN   FEB   MAR   APR   MAY   JUNE   JULY   AUG   SEPT   OCT   NOV   DEC

1 2 3 4 5 6 7 8 9 10 11 12 13 14 15 16 17 18 19 20 21 22 23 24 25 26 27 28 29 30 31

Daily Check-In

Mood:	Exercise: y n
Diet / Hydration:	Quiet time: y n
Energy level: *low--------------------------------high*	_____

The Struggles

The Growth & Overcoming

The Good List

Notes

Progress point

1. What is working well for me? What can I give myself credit for?

2. What did I try that didn't work well for me? Do I want to try to use it again or try a new tool?

3. What am I learning?

4. What is God revealing to me about Himself?

5. What goal or intention do I want to set moving forward?

6. What Bible verse, truth, or affirmation do I want to focus on?

S   M   T   W   T   F   S

JAN FEB MAR APR MAY JUNE JULY AUG SEPT OCT NOV DEC

1 2 3 4 5 6 7 8 9 10 11 12 13 14 15 16 17 18 19 20 21 22 23 24 25 26 27 28 29 30 31

Daily Check-In

Mood:	Exercise: y n
Diet / Hydration:	Quiet time: y n
Energy level: *low*-------------------------------*high*	_____

The Struggles

The Growth & Overcoming

The Good List

Notes

S   M   T   W   T   F   S

JAN   FEB   MAR   APR   MAY   JUNE   JULY   AUG   SEPT   OCT   NOV   DEC

1 2 3 4 5 6 7 8 9 10 11 12 13 14 15 16 17 18 19 20 21 22 23 24 25 26 27 28 29 30 31

Daily Check-In

Mood:	Exercise: y n
Diet / Hydration:	Quiet time: y n
Energy level: *low--------------------------------high*	_____

The Struggles

The Growth & Overcoming

The Good List

Notes

S M T W T F S

JAN FEB MAR APR MAY JUNE JULY AUG SEPT OCT NOV DEC

1 2 3 4 5 6 7 8 9 10 11 12 13 14 15 16 17 18 19 20 21 22 23 24 25 26 27 28 29 30 31

Daily Check-In

Mood:	Exercise: y n
Diet / Hydration:	Quiet time: y n
Energy level: *low------------------------------high*	_____

The Struggles

The Growth & Overcoming

The Good List

Notes

S   M   T   W   T   F   S

JAN FEB MAR APR MAY JUNE JULY AUG SEPT OCT NOV DEC

1 2 3 4 5 6 7 8 9 10 11 12 13 14 15 16 17 18 19 20 21 22 23 24 25 26 27 28 29 30 31

Daily Check-In

Mood:	Exercise: y n
Diet / Hydration:	Quiet time: y n
Energy level: *low-------------------------------high*	

The Struggles

The Growth & Overcoming

The Good List

Notes

S   M   T   W   T   F   S

JAN   FEB   MAR   APR   MAY   JUNE   JULY   AUG   SEPT   OCT   NOV   DEC

1 2 3 4 5 6 7 8 9 10 11 12 13 14 15 16 17 18 19 20 21 22 23 24 25 26 27 28 29 30 31

Daily Check-In

Mood:	Exercise: y n
Diet / Hydration:	Quiet time: y n
Energy level: *low*-------------------------------*high*	_____

The Struggles

The Growth & Overcoming

The Good List

Notes

S   M   T   W   T   F   S

JAN   FEB   MAR   APR   MAY   JUNE   JULY   AUG   SEPT   OCT   NOV   DEC

1   2   3   4   5   6   7   8   9   10   11   12   13   14   15   16   17   18   19   20   21   22   23   24   25   26   27   28   29   30   31

Daily Check-In

Mood:	Exercise: y n
Diet / Hydration:	Quiet time: y n
Energy level: *low*------------------------------*high*	

The Struggles

The Growth & Overcoming

The Good List

Notes

S   M   T   W   T   F   S

JAN FEB MAR APR MAY JUNE JULY AUG SEPT OCT NOV DEC

1 2 3 4 5 6 7 8 9 10 11 12 13 14 15 16 17 18 19 20 21 22 23 24 25 26 27 28 29 30 31

Daily Check-In

Mood:	Exercise:	y	n
Diet / Hydration:	Quiet time:	y	n
Energy level: *low---------------------------------high*			

The Struggles

The Growth & Overcoming

The Good List

Notes

S   M   T   W   T   F   S

JAN   FEB   MAR   APR   MAY   JUNE   JULY   AUG   SEPT   OCT   NOV   DEC

1 2 3 4 5 6 7 8 9 10 11 12 13 14 15 16 17 18 19 20 21 22 23 24 25 26 27 28 29 30 31

Daily Check-In

Mood:	Exercise:	y	n
Diet / Hydration:	Quiet time:	y	n
Energy level: *low*--------------------------------*high*			

The Struggles

The Growth & Overcoming

The Good List

Notes

S   M   T   W   T   F   S

JAN FEB MAR APR MAY JUNE JULY AUG SEPT OCT NOV DEC

1 2 3 4 5 6 7 8 9 10 11 12 13 14 15 16 17 18 19 20 21 22 23 24 25 26 27 28 29 30 31

Daily Check-In

Mood:	Exercise: y n
Diet / Hydration:	Quiet time: y n
Energy level: *low--------------------------------high*	_____

The Struggles

The Growth & Overcoming

The Good List

Notes

S   M   T   W   T   F   S

JAN   FEB   MAR   APR   MAY   JUNE   JULY   AUG   SEPT   OCT   NOV   DEC

1   2   3   4   5   6   7   8   9   10   11   12   13   14   15   16   17   18   19   20   21   22   23   24   25   26   27   28   29   30   31

Daily Check-In

Mood:	Exercise: y n
Diet / Hydration:	Quiet time: y n
Energy level: *low----------------------------------high*	_____

The Struggles

The Growth & Overcoming

The Good List

Notes

S   M   T   W   T   F   S

JAN   FEB   MAR   APR   MAY   JUNE   JULY   AUG   SEPT   OCT   NOV   DEC

1 2 3 4 5 6 7 8 9 10 11 12 13 14 15 16 17 18 19 20 21 22 23 24 25 26 27 28 29 30 31

Daily Check-In

Mood:	Exercise: y n
Diet / Hydration:	Quiet time: y n
Energy level: *low*-------------------------------*high*	_____

The Struggles

The Growth & Overcoming

The Good List

Notes

S   M   T   W   T   F   S

JAN   FEB   MAR   APR   MAY   JUNE   JULY   AUG   SEPT   OCT   NOV   DEC

1   2   3   4   5   6   7   8   9   10   11   12   13   14   15   16   17   18   19   20   21   22   23   24   25   26   27   28   29   30   31

Daily Check-In

Mood:	Exercise: y n
Diet / Hydration:	Quiet time: y n
Energy level: *low-------------------------------high*	_____

The Struggles

The Growth & Overcoming

The Good List

Notes

S   M   T   W   T   F   S

JAN   FEB   MAR   APR   MAY   JUNE   JULY   AUG   SEPT   OCT   NOV   DEC

1 2 3 4 5 6 7 8 9 10 11 12 13 14 15 16 17 18 19 20 21 22 23 24 25 26 27 28 29 30 31

Daily Check-In

Mood:	Exercise: y n
Diet / Hydration:	Quiet time: y n
Energy level: *low--------------------------------high*	_____

The Struggles

The Growth & Overcoming

The Good List

Notes

S	M	T	W	T	F	S

JAN   FEB   MAR   APR   MAY   JUNE   JULY   AUG   SEPT   OCT   NOV   DEC

1 2 3 4 5 6 7 8 9 10 11 12 13 14 15 16 17 18 19 20 21 22 23 24 25 26 27 28 29 30 31

Daily Check-In

Mood:	Exercise:	y	n
Diet / Hydration:	Quiet time:	y	n
Energy level: *low*-------------------------------*high*			

The Struggles

The Growth & Overcoming

The Good List

Notes

Progress point

1. What is working well for me? What can I give myself credit for?

2. What did I try that didn't work well for me? Do I want to try to use it again or try a new tool?

3. What am I learning?

4. What is God revealing to me about Himself?

5. What goal or intention do I want to set moving forward?

6. What Bible verse, truth, or affirmation do I want to focus on?

S   M   T   W   T   F   S

JAN   FEB   MAR   APR   MAY   JUNE   JULY   AUG   SEPT   OCT   NOV   DEC

1 2 3 4 5 6 7 8 9 10 11 12 13 14 15 16 17 18 19 20 21 22 23 24 25 26 27 28 29 30 31

Daily Check-In

Mood:	Exercise: y n
Diet / Hydration:	Quiet time: y n
Energy level: *low--------------------------------high*	_____

The Struggles

The Growth & Overcoming

The Good List

Notes

S   M   T   W   T   F   S

JAN   FEB   MAR   APR   MAY   JUNE   JULY   AUG   SEPT   OCT   NOV   DEC

1   2   3   4   5   6   7   8   9   10   11   12   13   14   15   16   17   18   19   20   21   22   23   24   25   26   27   28   29   30   31

Daily Check-In

Mood:	Exercise:　　　　　y　　　　n
Diet / Hydration:	Quiet time:　　　　　y　　　　n
Energy level: *low--------------------------------high*	_____

The Struggles

The Growth & Overcoming

The Good List

Notes

S   M   T   W   T   F   S

JAN   FEB   MAR   APR   MAY   JUNE   JULY   AUG   SEPT   OCT   NOV   DEC

1 2 3 4 5 6 7 8 9 10 11 12 13 14 15 16 17 18 19 20 21 22 23 24 25 26 27 28 29 30 31

Daily Check-In

Mood:	Exercise: y n
Diet / Hydration:	Quiet time: y n
Energy level: *low--------------------------------high*	_____

The Struggles

The Growth & Overcoming

The Good List

Notes

S   M   T   W   T   F   S

JAN   FEB   MAR   APR   MAY   JUNE   JULY   AUG   SEPT   OCT   NOV   DEC

1 2 3 4 5 6 7 8 9 10 11 12 13 14 15 16 17 18 19 20 21 22 23 24 25 26 27 28 29 30 31

Daily Check-In

Mood:	Exercise: y n
Diet / Hydration:	Quiet time: y n
Energy level: *low*-------------------------------*high*	_____

The Struggles

The Growth & Overcoming

The Good List

Notes

S M T W T F S

JAN FEB MAR APR MAY JUNE JULY AUG SEPT OCT NOV DEC

1 2 3 4 5 6 7 8 9 10 11 12 13 14 15 16 17 18 19 20 21 22 23 24 25 26 27 28 29 30 31

Daily Check-In

Mood:	Exercise: y n
Diet / Hydration:	Quiet time: y n
Energy level: *low*-------------------------------*high*	_____

The Struggles

The Growth & Overcoming

The Good List

Notes

S   M   T   W   T   F   S

JAN   FEB   MAR   APR   MAY   JUNE   JULY   AUG   SEPT   OCT   NOV   DEC

1 2 3 4 5 6 7 8 9 10 11 12 13 14 15 16 17 18 19 20 21 22 23 24 25 26 27 28 29 30 31

Daily Check-In

Mood:	Exercise: y n
Diet / Hydration:	Quiet time: y n
Energy level: *low*-------------------------------*high*	_____

The Struggles

The Growth & Overcoming

The Good List

Notes

	S		M		T		W		T		F		S

JAN   FEB   MAR   APR   MAY   JUNE   JULY   AUG   SEPT   OCT   NOV   DEC

1 2 3 4 5 6 7 8 9 10 11 12 13 14 15 16 17 18 19 20 21 22 23 24 25 26 27 28 29 30 31

Daily Check-In

Mood:	Exercise:	y	n
Diet / Hydration:	Quiet time:	y	n
Energy level: *low--------------------------------high*			

The Struggles

The Growth & Overcoming

The Good List

Notes

S   M   T   W   T   F   S

JAN   FEB   MAR   APR   MAY   JUNE   JULY   AUG   SEPT   OCT   NOV   DEC

1 2 3 4 5 6 7 8 9 10 11 12 13 14 15 16 17 18 19 20 21 22 23 24 25 26 27 28 29 30 31

Daily Check-In

Mood:	Exercise: y n
Diet / Hydration:	Quiet time: y n
Energy level: *low--------------------------------high*	_____

The Struggles

The Growth & Overcoming

The Good List

Notes

S   M   T   W   T   F   S

JAN   FEB   MAR   APR   MAY   JUNE   JULY   AUG   SEPT   OCT   NOV   DEC

1 2 3 4 5 6 7 8 9 10 11 12 13 14 15 16 17 18 19 20 21 22 23 24 25 26 27 28 29 30 31

Daily Check-In

Mood:	Exercise: y n
Diet / Hydration:	Quiet time: y n
Energy level: *low--------------------------------high*	_____

The Struggles

The Growth & Overcoming

The Good List

Notes

S   M   T   W   T   F   S

JAN   FEB   MAR   APR   MAY   JUNE   JULY   AUG   SEPT   OCT   NOV   DEC

1 2 3 4 5 6 7 8 9 10 11 12 13 14 15 16 17 18 19 20 21 22 23 24 25 26 27 28 29 30 31

Daily Check-In

Mood:	Exercise: y n
Diet / Hydration:	Quiet time: y n
Energy level: *low*-------------------------------*high*	_____

The Struggles

The Growth & Overcoming

The Good List

Notes

S M T W T F S

JAN FEB MAR APR MAY JUNE JULY AUG SEPT OCT NOV DEC
1 2 3 4 5 6 7 8 9 10 11 12 13 14 15 16 17 18 19 20 21 22 23 24 25 26 27 28 29 30 31

Daily Check-In

Mood:	Exercise: y n
Diet / Hydration:	Quiet time: y n
Energy level: *low*--------------------------------*high*	_____

The Struggles

The Growth & Overcoming

The Good List

Notes

S   M   T   W   T   F   S

JAN   FEB   MAR   APR   MAY   JUNE   JULY   AUG   SEPT   OCT   NOV   DEC

1   2   3   4   5   6   7   8   9   10   11   12   13   14   15   16   17   18   19   20   21   22   23   24   25   26   27   28   29   30   31

Daily Check-In

Mood:	Exercise: y n
Diet / Hydration:	Quiet time: y n
Energy level: *low--------------------------------high*	_____

The Struggles

The Growth & Overcoming

The Good List

Notes

S   M   T   W   T   F   S
JAN   FEB   MAR   APR   MAY   JUNE   JULY   AUG   SEPT   OCT   NOV   DEC
1 2 3 4 5 6 7 8 9 10 11 12 13 14 15 16 17 18 19 20 21 22 23 24 25 26 27 28 29 30 31

Daily Check-In

Mood:	Exercise: y n
Diet / Hydration:	Quiet time: y n
Energy level: *low------------------------------high*	_____

The Struggles

The Growth & Overcoming

The Good List

Notes

S   M   T   W   T   F   S

JAN   FEB   MAR   APR   MAY   JUNE   JULY   AUG   SEPT   OCT   NOV   DEC

1 2 3 4 5 6 7 8 9 10 11 12 13 14 15 16 17 18 19 20 21 22 23 24 25 26 27 28 29 30 31

Daily Check-In

Mood:	Exercise: y n
Diet / Hydration:	Quiet time: y n
Energy level: *low*-------------------------------*high*	_____

The Struggles

The Growth & Overcoming

The Good List

Notes

Progress point

1. What is working well for me? What can I give myself credit for?

2. What did I try that didn't work well for me? Do I want to try to use it again or try a new tool?

3. What am I learning?

4. What is God revealing to me about Himself?

5. What goal or intention do I want to set moving forward?

6. What Bible verse, truth, or affirmation do I want to focus on?

S M T W T F S

JAN FEB MAR APR MAY JUNE JULY AUG SEPT OCT NOV DEC

1 2 3 4 5 6 7 8 9 10 11 12 13 14 15 16 17 18 19 20 21 22 23 24 25 26 27 28 29 30 31

Daily Check-In

Mood:	Exercise: y n
Diet / Hydration:	Quiet time: y n
Energy level: *low--------------------------------high*	_____

The Struggles

The Growth & Overcoming

The Good List

Notes

S   M   T   W   T   F   S

JAN   FEB   MAR   APR   MAY   JUNE   JULY   AUG   SEPT   OCT   NOV   DEC

1   2   3   4   5   6   7   8   9   10   11   12   13   14   15   16   17   18   19   20   21   22   23   24   25   26   27   28   29   30   31

Daily Check-In

Mood:	Exercise: y n
Diet / Hydration:	Quiet time: y n
Energy level: *low--------------------------------high*	

The Struggles

The Growth & Overcoming

The Good List

Notes

S   M   T   W   T   F   S

JAN   FEB   MAR   APR   MAY   JUNE   JULY   AUG   SEPT   OCT   NOV   DEC

1 2 3 4 5 6 7 8 9 10 11 12 13 14 15 16 17 18 19 20 21 22 23 24 25 26 27 28 29 30 31

Daily Check-In

Mood:	Exercise: y n
Diet / Hydration:	Quiet time: y n
Energy level: *low*-----------------------------*high*	_____

The Struggles

The Growth & Overcoming

The Good List

Notes

S   M   T   W   T   F   S

JAN FEB MAR APR MAY JUNE JULY AUG SEPT OCT NOV DEC

1 2 3 4 5 6 7 8 9 10 11 12 13 14 15 16 17 18 19 20 21 22 23 24 25 26 27 28 29 30 31

Daily Check-In

Mood:		Exercise:	y n
Diet / Hydration:		Quiet time:	y n
Energy level: *low--------------------------------high*			

The Struggles

The Growth & Overcoming

The Good List

Notes

S M T W T F S

JAN FEB MAR APR MAY JUNE JULY AUG SEPT OCT NOV DEC

1 2 3 4 5 6 7 8 9 10 11 12 13 14 15 16 17 18 19 20 21 22 23 24 25 26 27 28 29 30 31

Daily Check-In

Mood:	Exercise: y n
Diet / Hydration:	Quiet time: y n
Energy level: *low*-------------------------------*high*	

The Struggles

The Growth & Overcoming

The Good List

Notes

S   M   T   W   T   F   S

JAN FEB MAR APR MAY JUNE JULY AUG SEPT OCT NOV DEC

1 2 3 4 5 6 7 8 9 10 11 12 13 14 15 16 17 18 19 20 21 22 23 24 25 26 27 28 29 30 31

Daily Check-In

Mood:	Exercise: y n
Diet / Hydration:	Quiet time: y n
Energy level: *low--------------------------------high*	_____

The Struggles

The Growth & Overcoming

The Good List

Notes

S   M   T   W   T   F   S

JAN FEB MAR APR MAY JUNE JULY AUG SEPT OCT NOV DEC

1 2 3 4 5 6 7 8 9 10 11 12 13 14 15 16 17 18 19 20 21 22 23 24 25 26 27 28 29 30 31

Daily Check-In

Mood:	Exercise:	y	n
Diet / Hydration:	Quiet time:	y	n
Energy level: *low*------------------------------*high*			

The Struggles

The Growth & Overcoming

The Good List

Notes

S   M   T   W   T   F   S

JAN   FEB   MAR   APR   MAY   JUNE   JULY   AUG   SEPT   OCT   NOV   DEC

1 2 3 4 5 6 7 8 9 10 11 12 13 14 15 16 17 18 19 20 21 22 23 24 25 26 27 28 29 30 31

Daily Check-In

Mood:	Exercise: y n
Diet / Hydration:	Quiet time: y n
Energy level: *low--------------------------------high*	_____

The Struggles

The Growth & Overcoming

The Good List

Notes

| S | M | T | W | T | F | S |

JAN   FEB   MAR   APR   MAY   JUNE   JULY   AUG   SEPT   OCT   NOV   DEC
1   2   3   4   5   6   7   8   9   10   11   12   13   14   15   16   17   18   19   20   21   22   23   24   25   26   27   28   29   30   31

Daily Check-In

Mood:	Exercise: y n
Diet / Hydration:	Quiet time: y n
Energy level: *low---------------------------------high*	_____

The Struggles

The Growth & Overcoming

The Good List

Notes

S   M   T   W   T   F   S

JAN FEB MAR APR MAY JUNE JULY AUG SEPT OCT NOV DEC

1 2 3 4 5 6 7 8 9 10 11 12 13 14 15 16 17 18 19 20 21 22 23 24 25 26 27 28 29 30 31

Daily Check-In

Mood:	Exercise: y n
Diet / Hydration:	Quiet time: y n
Energy level: *low--------------------------------high*	_____

The Struggles

The Growth & Overcoming

The Good List

Notes

S   M   T   W   T   F   S

JAN   FEB   MAR   APR   MAY   JUNE   JULY   AUG   SEPT   OCT   NOV   DEC

1   2   3   4   5   6   7   8   9   10   11   12   13   14   15   16   17   18   19   20   21   22   23   24   25   26   27   28   29   30   31

Daily Check-In

Mood:	Exercise: y n
Diet / Hydration:	Quiet time: y n
Energy level: *low*------------------------------*high*	_____

The Struggles

The Growth & Overcoming

The Good List

Notes

S	M	T	W	T	F	S

JAN   FEB   MAR   APR   MAY   JUNE   JULY   AUG   SEPT   OCT   NOV   DEC

1 2 3 4 5 6 7 8 9 10 11 12 13 14 15 16 17 18 19 20 21 22 23 24 25 26 27 28 29 30 31

Daily Check-In

Mood:	Exercise: y n
Diet / Hydration:	Quiet time: y n
Energy level: *low*-------------------------------*high*	_____

The Struggles

The Growth & Overcoming

The Good List

Notes

S   M   T   W   T   F   S

JAN   FEB   MAR   APR   MAY   JUNE   JULY   AUG   SEPT   OCT   NOV   DEC

1 2 3 4 5 6 7 8 9 10 11 12 13 14 15 16 17 18 19 20 21 22 23 24 25 26 27 28 29 30 31

Daily Check-In

Mood:	Exercise:	y	n
Diet / Hydration:	Quiet time:	y	n
Energy level: *low--------------------------------high*			

The Struggles

The Growth & Overcoming

The Good List

Notes

S   M   T   W   T   F   S

JAN   FEB   MAR   APR   MAY   JUNE   JULY   AUG   SEPT   OCT   NOV   DEC

1 2 3 4 5 6 7 8 9 10 11 12 13 14 15 16 17 18 19 20 21 22 23 24 25 26 27 28 29 30 31

Daily Check-In

Mood:	Exercise:	y n
Diet / Hydration:	Quiet time:	y n
Energy level: *low--------------------------------high*		

The Struggles

The Growth & Overcoming

The Good List

Notes

Progress point

1. What is working well for me? What can I give myself credit for?

2. What did I try that didn't work well for me? Do I want to try to use it again or try a new tool?

3. What am I learning?

4. What is God revealing to me about Himself?

5. What goal or intention do I want to set moving forward?

6. What Bible verse, truth, or affirmation do I want to focus on?

S M T W T F S

JAN FEB MAR APR MAY JUNE JULY AUG SEPT OCT NOV DEC

1 2 3 4 5 6 7 8 9 10 11 12 13 14 15 16 17 18 19 20 21 22 23 24 25 26 27 28 29 30 31

Daily Check-In

Mood:	Exercise: y n
Diet / Hydration:	Quiet time: y n
Energy level: *low*------------------------------*high*	_____

The Struggles

The Growth & Overcoming

The Good List

Notes

S   M   T   W   T   F   S

JAN FEB MAR APR MAY JUNE JULY AUG SEPT OCT NOV DEC

1 2 3 4 5 6 7 8 9 10 11 12 13 14 15 16 17 18 19 20 21 22 23 24 25 26 27 28 29 30 31

Daily Check-In

Mood:	Exercise: y n
Diet / Hydration:	Quiet time: y n
Energy level: *low--------------------------------high*	_____

The Struggles

The Growth & Overcoming

The Good List

Notes

S   M   T   W   T   F   S

JAN   FEB   MAR   APR   MAY   JUNE   JULY   AUG   SEPT   OCT   NOV   DEC

1 2 3 4 5 6 7 8 9 10 11 12 13 14 15 16 17 18 19 20 21 22 23 24 25 26 27 28 29 30 31

Daily Check-In

Mood:	Exercise: y n
Diet / Hydration:	Quiet time: y n
Energy level: *low*---------------------------------*high*	_____

The Struggles

The Growth & Overcoming

The Good List

Notes

S   M   T   W   T   F   S

JAN   FEB   MAR   APR   MAY   JUNE   JULY   AUG   SEPT   OCT   NOV   DEC

1 2 3 4 5 6 7 8 9 10 11 12 13 14 15 16 17 18 19 20 21 22 23 24 25 26 27 28 29 30 31

Daily Check-In

Mood:	Exercise: y n
Diet / Hydration:	Quiet time: y n
Energy level: *low*-------------------------------*high*	_____

The Struggles

The Growth & Overcoming

The Good List

Notes

S   M   T   W   T   F   S

JAN   FEB   MAR   APR   MAY   JUNE   JULY   AUG   SEPT   OCT   NOV   DEC

1 2 3 4 5 6 7 8 9 10 11 12 13 14 15 16 17 18 19 20 21 22 23 24 25 26 27 28 29 30 31

Daily Check-In

Mood:	Exercise: y n
Diet / Hydration:	Quiet time: y n
Energy level: *low--------------------------------high*	_____

The Struggles

The Growth & Overcoming

The Good List

Notes

S   M   T   W   T   F   S

JAN FEB MAR APR MAY JUNE JULY AUG SEPT OCT NOV DEC

1 2 3 4 5 6 7 8 9 10 11 12 13 14 15 16 17 18 19 20 21 22 23 24 25 26 27 28 29 30 31

Daily Check-In

Mood:	Exercise: y n
Diet / Hydration:	Quiet time: y n
Energy level: *low*-------------------------------*high*	_____

The Struggles

The Growth & Overcoming

The Good List

Notes

S   M   T   W   T   F   S

JAN FEB MAR APR MAY JUNE JULY AUG SEPT OCT NOV DEC

1 2 3 4 5 6 7 8 9 10 11 12 13 14 15 16 17 18 19 20 21 22 23 24 25 26 27 28 29 30 31

Daily Check-In

Mood:	Exercise: y n
Diet / Hydration:	Quiet time: y n
Energy level: *low------------------------------high*	_____

The Struggles

The Growth & Overcoming

The Good List

Notes

S M T W T F S
JAN FEB MAR APR MAY JUNE JULY AUG SEPT OCT NOV DEC
1 2 3 4 5 6 7 8 9 10 11 12 13 14 15 16 17 18 19 20 21 22 23 24 25 26 27 28 29 30 31

Daily Check-In

Mood:	Exercise: y n
Diet / Hydration:	Quiet time: y n
Energy level: *low--------------------------------high*	_____

The Struggles

The Growth & Overcoming

The Good List

Notes

S   M   T   W   T   F   S

JAN   FEB   MAR   APR   MAY   JUNE   JULY   AUG   SEPT   OCT   NOV   DEC
1 2 3 4 5 6 7 8 9 10 11 12 13 14 15 16 17 18 19 20 21 22 23 24 25 26 27 28 29 30 31

Daily Check-In

Mood:	Exercise: y n
Diet / Hydration:	Quiet time: y n
Energy level: *low--------------------------------high*	

The Struggles

The Growth & Overcoming

The Good List

Notes

S M T W T F S

JAN FEB MAR APR MAY JUNE JULY AUG SEPT OCT NOV DEC

1 2 3 4 5 6 7 8 9 10 11 12 13 14 15 16 17 18 19 20 21 22 23 24 25 26 27 28 29 30 31

Daily Check-In

Mood:	Exercise: y n
Diet / Hydration:	Quiet time: y n
Energy level: *low*------------------------------*high*	_____

The Struggles

The Growth & Overcoming

The Good List

Notes

S   M   T   W   T   F   S

JAN   FEB   MAR   APR   MAY   JUNE   JULY   AUG   SEPT   OCT   NOV   DEC

1 2 3 4 5 6 7 8 9 10 11 12 13 14 15 16 17 18 19 20 21 22 23 24 25 26 27 28 29 30 31

Daily Check-In

Mood:
Diet / Hydration:
Energy level: *low--------------------------------high*

Exercise: y   n
Quiet time: y   n
_____

The Struggles

The Growth & Overcoming

The Good List

Notes

S   M   T   W   T   F   S

JAN   FEB   MAR   APR   MAY   JUNE   JULY   AUG   SEPT   OCT   NOV   DEC

1 2 3 4 5 6 7 8 9 10 11 12 13 14 15 16 17 18 19 20 21 22 23 24 25 26 27 28 29 30 31

Daily Check-In

Mood:	Exercise:　　　　y　　　　n
Diet / Hydration:	Quiet time:　　　　y　　　　n
Energy level: *low*-----------------------------*high*	_____

The Struggles

The Growth & Overcoming

The Good List

Notes

S   M   T   W   T   F   S

JAN   FEB   MAR   APR   MAY   JUNE   JULY   AUG   SEPT   OCT   NOV   DEC

1 2 3 4 5 6 7 8 9 10 11 12 13 14 15 16 17 18 19 20 21 22 23 24 25 26 27 28 29 30 31

Daily Check-In

Mood:	Exercise: y n
Diet / Hydration:	Quiet time: y n
Energy level: *low-------------------------------high*	_____

The Struggles

The Growth & Overcoming

The Good List

Notes

S   M   T   W   T   F   S

JAN FEB MAR APR MAY JUNE JULY AUG SEPT OCT NOV DEC

1 2 3 4 5 6 7 8 9 10 11 12 13 14 15 16 17 18 19 20 21 22 23 24 25 26 27 28 29 30 31

Daily Check-In

Mood:	Exercise: y n
Diet / Hydration:	Quiet time: y n
Energy level: *low*-------------------------------*high*	

The Struggles

The Growth & Overcoming

The Good List

Notes

Progress point

1. What is working well for me? What can I give myself credit for?

2. What did I try that didn't work well for me? Do I want to try to use it again or try a new tool?

3. What am I learning?

4. What is God revealing to me about Himself?

5. What goal or intention do I want to set moving forward?

6. What Bible verse, truth, or affirmation do I want to focus on?

S   M   T   W   T   F   S

JAN FEB MAR APR MAY JUNE JULY AUG SEPT OCT NOV DEC

1 2 3 4 5 6 7 8 9 10 11 12 13 14 15 16 17 18 19 20 21 22 23 24 25 26 27 28 29 30 31

Daily Check-In

Mood:	Exercise: y n
Diet / Hydration:	Quiet time: y n
Energy level: *low-------------------------------high*	_____

The Struggles

The Growth & Overcoming

The Good List

Notes

S   M   T   W   T   F   S

JAN   FEB   MAR   APR   MAY   JUNE   JULY   AUG   SEPT   OCT   NOV   DEC

1 2 3 4 5 6 7 8 9 10 11 12 13 14 15 16 17 18 19 20 21 22 23 24 25 26 27 28 29 30 31

Daily Check-In

Mood:	Exercise:	y n
Diet / Hydration:	Quiet time:	y n
Energy level: *low------------------------------high*		

The Struggles

The Growth & Overcoming

The Good List

Notes

S	M	T	W	T	F	S

JAN   FEB   MAR   APR   MAY   JUNE   JULY   AUG   SEPT   OCT   NOV   DEC

1 2 3 4 5 6 7 8 9 10 11 12 13 14 15 16 17 18 19 20 21 22 23 24 25 26 27 28 29 30 31

Daily Check-In

Mood:	Exercise: y n
Diet / Hydration:	Quiet time: y n
Energy level: *low--------------------------------high*	

The Struggles

The Growth & Overcoming

The Good List

Notes

S   M   T   W   T   F   S

JAN FEB MAR APR MAY JUNE JULY AUG SEPT OCT NOV DEC

1 2 3 4 5 6 7 8 9 10 11 12 13 14 15 16 17 18 19 20 21 22 23 24 25 26 27 28 29 30 31

Daily Check-In

Mood:	Exercise:	y	n
Diet / Hydration:	Quiet time:	y	n
Energy level: *low--------------------------------high*			

The Struggles

The Growth & Overcoming

The Good List

Notes

S   M   T   W   T   F   S

JAN FEB MAR APR MAY JUNE JULY AUG SEPT OCT NOV DEC

1 2 3 4 5 6 7 8 9 10 11 12 13 14 15 16 17 18 19 20 21 22 23 24 25 26 27 28 29 30 31

Daily Check-In

Mood:	Exercise: y n
Diet / Hydration:	Quiet time: y n
Energy level: *low*-------------------------------*high*	_____

The Struggles

The Growth & Overcoming

The Good List

Notes

| S | M | T | W | T | F | S |

JAN FEB MAR APR MAY JUNE JULY AUG SEPT OCT NOV DEC

1 2 3 4 5 6 7 8 9 10 11 12 13 14 15 16 17 18 19 20 21 22 23 24 25 26 27 28 29 30 31

Daily Check-In

Mood:	Exercise:	y	n
Diet / Hydration:	Quiet time:	y	n
Energy level: *low---------------------------------high*			

The Struggles

The Growth & Overcoming

The Good List

Notes

S M T W T F S

JAN FEB MAR APR MAY JUNE JULY AUG SEPT OCT NOV DEC

1 2 3 4 5 6 7 8 9 10 11 12 13 14 15 16 17 18 19 20 21 22 23 24 25 26 27 28 29 30 31

Daily Check-In

Mood:	Exercise: y n
Diet / Hydration:	Quiet time: y n
Energy level: *low--------------------------------high*	_____

The Struggles

The Growth & Overcoming

The Good List

Notes

S   M   T   W   T   F   S

JAN FEB MAR APR MAY JUNE JULY AUG SEPT OCT NOV DEC

1 2 3 4 5 6 7 8 9 10 11 12 13 14 15 16 17 18 19 20 21 22 23 24 25 26 27 28 29 30 31

Daily Check-In

Mood:	Exercise:	y	n
Diet / Hydration:	Quiet time:	y	n
Energy level: *low--------------------------------high*			

The Struggles

The Growth & Overcoming

The Good List

Notes

S M T W T F S

JAN FEB MAR APR MAY JUNE JULY AUG SEPT OCT NOV DEC

1 2 3 4 5 6 7 8 9 10 11 12 13 14 15 16 17 18 19 20 21 22 23 24 25 26 27 28 29 30 31

Daily Check-In

Mood:	Exercise: y n
Diet / Hydration:	Quiet time: y n
Energy level: *low------------------------------high*	_____

The Struggles

The Growth & Overcoming

The Good List

Notes

S   M   T   W   T   F   S

JAN FEB MAR APR MAY JUNE JULY AUG SEPT OCT NOV DEC

1 2 3 4 5 6 7 8 9 10 11 12 13 14 15 16 17 18 19 20 21 22 23 24 25 26 27 28 29 30 31

Daily Check-In

Mood:	Exercise: y n
Diet / Hydration:	Quiet time: y n
Energy level: *low--------------------------------high*	_____

The Struggles

The Growth & Overcoming

The Good List

Notes

S   M   T   W   T   F   S

JAN   FEB   MAR   APR   MAY   JUNE   JULY   AUG   SEPT   OCT   NOV   DEC

1 2 3 4 5 6 7 8 9 10 11 12 13 14 15 16 17 18 19 20 21 22 23 24 25 26 27 28 29 30 31

Daily Check-In

Mood:	Exercise: y n
Diet / Hydration:	Quiet time: y n
Energy level: *low*-------------------------------*high*	_____

The Struggles

The Growth & Overcoming

The Good List

Notes

S M T W T F S

JAN FEB MAR APR MAY JUNE JULY AUG SEPT OCT NOV DEC

1 2 3 4 5 6 7 8 9 10 11 12 13 14 15 16 17 18 19 20 21 22 23 24 25 26 27 28 29 30 31

Daily Check-In

Mood:	Exercise: y n
Diet / Hydration:	Quiet time: y n
Energy level: *low--------------------------------high*	_____

The Struggles

The Growth & Overcoming

The Good List

Notes

S   M   T   W   T   F   S

JAN   FEB   MAR   APR   MAY   JUNE   JULY   AUG   SEPT   OCT   NOV   DEC
1 2 3 4 5 6 7 8 9 10 11 12 13 14 15 16 17 18 19 20 21 22 23 24 25 26 27 28 29 30 31

Daily Check-In

Mood:	Exercise: y n
Diet / Hydration:	Quiet time: y n
Energy level: *low*------------------------------*high*	_____

The Struggles

The Growth & Overcoming

The Good List

Notes

S M T W T F S
JAN FEB MAR APR MAY JUNE JULY AUG SEPT OCT NOV DEC
1 2 3 4 5 6 7 8 9 10 11 12 13 14 15 16 17 18 19 20 21 22 23 24 25 26 27 28 29 30 31

Daily Check-In

Mood:	Exercise: y n
Diet / Hydration:	Quiet time: y n
Energy level: *low-------------------------------high*	

The Struggles

The Growth & Overcoming

The Good List

Notes

Progress point

1. What is working well for me? What can I give myself credit for?

2. What did I try that didn't work well for me? Do I want to try to use it again or try a new tool?

3. What am I learning?

4. What is God revealing to me about Himself?

5. What goal or intention do I want to set moving forward?

6. What Bible verse, truth, or affirmation do I want to focus on?

Revelations

Revelations

Revelations

Revelations

Revelations

Revelations

Revelations

Revelations

Revelations

Revelations

Revelations

Revelations

Revelations

Revelations

Revelations

Revelations

Revelations

Revelations

Revelations

Revelations

Revelations

Revelations

Revelations

Revelations

Revelations

Revelations

Revelations

Revelations

Revelations

Revelations

Revelations

Revelations

Revelations

Revelations

Revelations

Revelations

Revelations

Revelations

Revelations

Revelations

Revelations

Revelations

Revelations

Revelations

Revelations

Revelations

Revelations

Revelations

Revelations

Revelations

Revelations

Revelations

Revelations

Revelations

Revelations

Revelations

Revelations

Revelations

Revelations

Revelations

Revelations

Revelations

Revelations

Revelations

Revelations

Revelations

Revelations

Revelations

Revelations

Revelations

Revelations

Revelations

Additional recommended resources:

Download a free PDF list of book recommendations from Kristin to help you with your journey of coming alive to your life and finding growth and overcoming with God. Visit:

www.KristinVanderlip.com/resources

Are you interested in a journal like this for kids? Learn more about Kristin's journal: *Living Life Well: A Daily Growth Journal for Kids*. Available exclusively on Amazon!

www.KristinVanderlip.com/journalforkids

About Kristin Vanderlip

Kristin is an ordinary woman who has known the depths of suffering and despair and knows what it's like to struggle having experienced the deaths of her first child and father as well as through her daily life as an Army wife. Kristin has learned how to pursue God in the midst of pain and discover her own life worth living. She uses her words to help women find hope and live in expectation of God's promises in the midst of unexpected pain and suffering. She writes regularly at www.kristinvanderlip.com and has had her words featured online at (in)courage, For Every Mom, and Women Encouraged as well as in the print magazine *iola*. Kristin, her husband, and their two boys call home wherever the Army sends them.

To learn more about Kristin and connect with her online visit:

www.KristinVanderlip.com

www.instagram.com/KristinVanderlip

www.facebook.com/kristinvanderlipwriter

Made in the USA
Coppell, TX
23 November 2019